DISCOVER!

ANIMALS THAT SLITHER AND SLIDE

CRAWLING CENTIPEDES

Enslow PUBLISHING

BY THERESA EMMINIZER

Please visit our website, www.enslow.com. For a free color catalog of all our high-quality books, call toll free 1-800-398-2504 or fax 1-877-980-4454.

Library of Congress Cataloging-in-Publication Data

Names: Emminizer, Theresa, author.
Title: Crawling centipedes / Theresa Emminizer.
Description: Buffalo : Enslow Publishing, [2024] | Series: Animals that slither and slide | Includes index. | Audience: Grades K-1
Identifiers: LCCN 2023027906 (print) | LCCN 2023027907 (ebook) | ISBN 9781978537293 (library binding) | ISBN 9781978537286 (paperback) | ISBN 9781978537309 (ebook)
Subjects: LCSH: Centipedes–Juvenile literature.
Classification: LCC QL449.5 .E46 2024 (print) | LCC QL449.5 (ebook) | DDC 595.6/2–dc23/eng/20230713
LC record available at https://lccn.loc.gov/2023027906
LC ebook record available at https://lccn.loc.gov/2023027907

First Edition

Published in 2024 by
Enslow Publishing
2544 Clinton Street
Buffalo, NY 14224

Copyright © 2024 Enslow Publishing

Designer: Leslie Taylor
Editor: Theresa Emminizer

Photo credits: Cover (centipede) skifbook/Shutterstock.com, (slime background) AMarc/Shutterstock.com, (brush stroke) Sonic_S/Shutterstock.com, (slime frame) klyaksun/Shutterstock.com; Series Art (slime blob) Lemberg Vector studio/Shutterstock.com; p. 5 Jolypics/Shutterstock.com; p.7 Ivan Marjanovic/Shutterstock.com; p.9 Lutsenko_Oleksandr/Shutterstock.com; p.11 CPbackpacker/Shutterstock.com; p.13 Kristi Blokhin/Shutterstock.com; p.15 kooanan007/Shutterstock.com; p.17 WITSANU PORNSUKNIMITKUL/Shutterstock.com; p.19 RealityImages/Shutterstock.com; p.21 (centipede) SUCHARUT CHOUNYOO/Shutterstock.com, (millipede) CJansuebsri/Shutterstock.com.

All rights reserved. No part of this book may be reproduced in any form without permission in writing from the publisher, except by a reviewer.

Some of the images in this book illustrate individuals who are models. The depictions do not imply actual situations or events.

Printed in the United States of America

CPSIA compliance information: Batch #CW24ENS: For further information contact Enslow Publishing, at 1-800-398-2504.

CONTENTS

What's That? 4
Creepy Feet! 6
Not a Bug 8
Where Do They Live? 10
The Smallest Centipede 12
The Biggest Centipede 14
What Do They Eat? 16
Life of a Centipede 18
Fast and Deadly 20
Words to Know 22
For More Information 23
Index 24

Boldface words appear in
Words to Know.

WHAT'S THAT?

Picture yourself playing outside. You're having fun digging in the dirt, shoveling it here, dropping it there. You pick up a rock. Underneath you see a long, shiny critter with too many legs to count! What on Earth is it? A centipede!

Centipedes like to hide under rocks.

CREEPY FEET!

The name "centipede" suggests that this animal has 100 feet. In fact, centipedes can have anywhere from about 14 to 177 pairs of legs. Centipedes' legs are placed on the sides of their bodies, not underneath. This helps them move faster!

Centipede means "100 foot" in Latin.

NOT A BUG

Centipedes aren't **insects**, they're arthropods. That means they have an exoskeleton, or hard outer shell, and their bodies are made of segments, or parts. Each segment (except the last) has a pair of legs. They also have **antennae** and sometimes claws!

House centipedes have legs that can detach, or come off!

WHERE DO THEY LIVE?

Centipedes live all around the world. There are around 3,000 known species, or kinds, of centipedes! Centipedes like to be in places that are cool, **damp**, and dark. They're often found in caves, under rocks, or underground.

CAVE CENTIPEDE

11

THE SMALLEST CENTIPEDE

The smallest kind of centipede is called the Hoffman's **dwarf** centipede. It's short at only 0.4 inch (10 mm) long. It has 41 pairs of legs. It was first found in Central Park, New York City, in 1998 and named in 2002.

THE BIGGEST CENTIPEDE

Giant centipedes are the biggest centipede species. They're up to about 1 foot (30 cm) long and have 23 pairs of legs. They also have **venomous** claws! The giant centipede's bite usually can't kill a person, but it's painful and can make you sick.

Giant centipedes are nocturnal. That means they only come out at night.

WHAT DO THEY EAT?

Most centipedes eat spiders, worms, and bugs. The largest species may also eat mice, lizards, and frogs. Some even kill birds! Centipedes use their many legs to catch and hold **prey**. Some have hooklike legs and **pincers**.

Here, a centipede catches a frog.

17

LIFE OF A CENTIPEDE

Female centipedes lay eggs. The eggs are covered in sticky stuff and dirt. Young centipedes start out with four pairs of legs. As they grow, they shed, or lose, their exoskeleton, and more segments and legs are added to their bodies.

A centipede mother and her eggs.

19

FAST AND DEADLY

What's the difference between a centipede and a millipede? Millipedes are usually smaller and slower than centipedes. Centipedes can run as fast as 16 inches (41 cm) per second. That's about the same as a person running 42 miles (68 km) per hour!

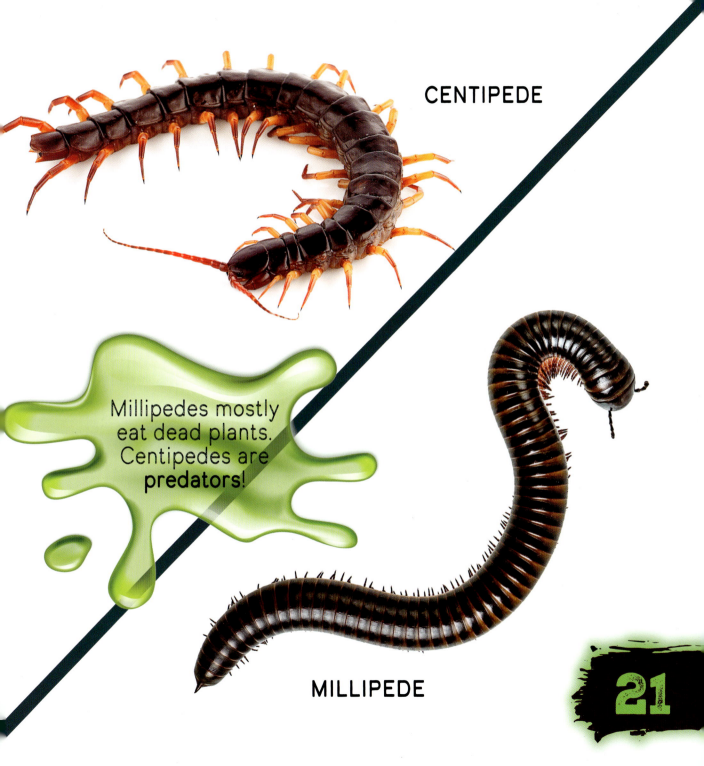

WORDS TO KNOW

antenna: A feeler on the head of some animals. The plural of "antenna" is "antennae."

damp: Somewhat wet.

dwarf: A word to describe things that are smaller than a usual size.

insect: A small, often winged, animal with six legs and three main body parts.

leaf litter: Plant matter that has fallen to the ground in a pile.

pincer: A front claw on some animals that is used to hold things.

predator: An animal that hunts other animals for food.

prey: An animal that is hunted by other animals for food.

venomous: Able to produce a liquid called venom that is harmful to other animals.

FOR MORE INFORMATION

BOOKS

Becker, Trudy. *Centipedes*. Lake Elmo, MN: Focus Readers, 2023.

Spikol, Susie. *The Animal Adventurer's Guide*. Boulder, CO: Roost Books, 2022.

WEBSITES

Centipede and Millipede
kids.britannica.com/kids/article/Centipede-andMillipede/399396
Find out more about centipedes and millipedes!

Sciencing
sciencing.com/centipede-kids-8527849.html
Learn more fun facts about centipedes!

Publisher's note to educators and parents: Our editors have carefully reviewed these websites to ensure that they are suitable for students. Many websites change frequently, however, and we cannot guarantee that a site's future contents will continue to meet our high standards of quality and educational value. Be advised that students should be closely supervised whenever they access the internet.

INDEX

cave, 10, 11

claws, 8, 14

eggs, 18, 19

exoskeleton, 8, 18

food, 16, 21

giant centipede, 14, 15

Hoffman's dwarf
  centipede, 12, 13

house centipede, 9

legs, 4, 6, 8, 9, 12,
  14, 16, 18

millipede, 20, 21

rocks, 4, 5, 10

segments, 8, 18

species, 10, 14, 16

speed, 6, 20